Assembly Instructions

Mounting on Cardboard

This book contains material for a complete Plains Indians diorama, including backgrounds for two different settings. The first background shows a tepee camp; it will be glued in place. The second background shows the setting for a buffalo hunt; you must add tabs at the top (see below) so that it may be dropped over the first background and removed as you wish.

To make the diorama durable, mount the following pieces on lightweight cardboard (such as oaktag): front panel, first background (showing the tepee camp), outer right side, outer left side, floor. For the pages containing the front panel and the outer side panels, be sure to cut away the pieces that are not to be glued onto cardboard (cutout stand-up figures; inner side panels).

For mounting, use a white glue such as Elmer's Glue-All. It dries very quickly, so you must work rapidly. Spread the glue over the cardboard (not over the paper). You can achieve an even coating by pouring the glue onto the surface and spreading the glue evenly with a squeegee made of a $2'' \times 4''$ piece of cardboard. Place the unprinted side of each piece to be glued on the cardboard and press down, using a clean $2'' \times 4''$ cardboard squeegee to remove any air pockets or wrinkles. Take care to prevent the glue from spreading onto the printed side; keep a wet sponge or damp rag handy to wipe away excess glue if necessary. Once you have spread the piece onto the cardboard and checked to see that there is no glue on the printed side, position a sheet of waxed paper over the piece, then place a weight, such as a heavy book, on top of it. Set aside for at least 15 minutes or until the glue has dried.

To cut out the individual pieces, use an X-Acto knife or matt knife and a steel-edged ruler. If you have never used an X-Acto knife, be careful; the blade is extremely sharp! Practice using the knife on scrap cardboard first. To protect your table or desk, prepare a disposable work surface on which to cut out the pieces, since you will be cutting completely through the cardboard mounting. Use a large sheet of plywood or heavy cardboard;

hold it in position with a pair of lightweight C-clamps or wood clips to prevent slippage while cutting. The outer side pieces can be carefully cut along the solid black lines using a pair of large scissors.

Hints

Read through all the instructions carefully before beginning the assembly, then follow the instructions in the exact order given. Before gluing any of the parts together, check for proper positioning and fit. Follow the exploded Diorama Assembly Diagram for proper orientation of the pieces. The colored sides of the front panel and of the outer side panels face outward.

Scoring

Gently score the broken fold lines on the floor and the outer side panels by lightly tracing the lines with an X-Acto knife held against a metal-edged ruler. Score lines should not cut through the piece more than halfway. Bend the pieces gently along the score lines so the floor stands on its braces and so the blank sides of the outer side panels are on the inside of the "U" thus formed.

Assembly

With blank surfaces facing one another, glue the inner left side to the outer left side between the scored fold lines; keep the top and bottom edges flush. Repeat for the right side. Let dry.

Glue the front (left-hand) flap of the outer left side to the *wrong* side of the front panel, making a 90° angle at the corner. Glue the back (right-hand) flap of the outer left side *behind* the first background as shown in the assembly diagram. Glue the front (right-hand) flap of the outer right side to the wrong side of the front panel, and the back (left-hand) flap behind the first background. Spread glue over the braces of the floor, position the diorama over the floor and gently lower it into position, making sure that all bottom edges are flush; glue front brace to back of front panel, and back brace to front of background. Let dry thoroughly.

The second background (for the buffalo hunt) is designed to be dropped in place inside the diorama so that it covers the fixed background. Secure it by pasting or taping two small tabs of plain heavy paper (you may use waste scraps from this book) to the back at the top, and bending them back over the fixed background. If you wish, you may add an extra piece of tape to each tab to hold them in place.

DIORAMA ASSEMBLY DIAGRAM

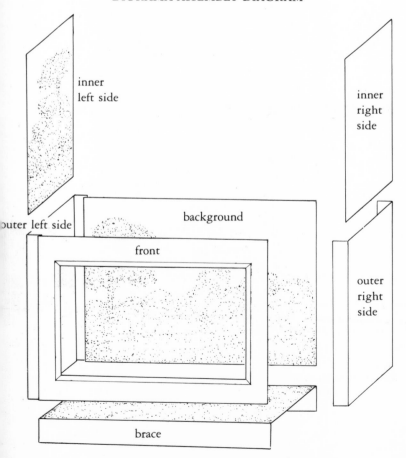

TAB ASSEMBLY DIAGRAM

Cutouts of Individuals, Groups, and Objects

Using a pair of curved cuticle scissors or very fine straight scissors, cut around the shapes. For complicated areas that may be too fragile if cut closely, leave the shaded background areas in place. After the entire piece has been cut, including the tabs, bend the tabs along the dashed fold lines. Follow the Tab Assembly Diagram to overlap the tabs; this will enable the cutouts to stand securely. Glue or tape the overlapped tabs together for added security.

For some of the larger cutouts, the tabs will not be long enough to overlap one another at the back; these cutouts will stand simply by bending the tabs along the fold lines as for the smaller cutouts. If desired, cut a ¼"-wide strip of waste paper from this book and tape or glue to the tabs of the larger cutouts. Overlap and secure as described above.

The Plains Indians of North America

They thunder over endless rolling plains under the vast Dakota sky. Innumerable Indians riding galloping steeds—their bright ornaments glistening in the sun, the feathers in their hair and fringes on their leggings flying in the wind—swoop over a grassy ridge. Their plumed spears and bows and arrows, their fiercely painted faces and loud whoops bode ill for enemies or the unwary buffalo.

These are the Indians of the Great Plains—the only Indians familiar to many of us today, thanks to Western fiction and films and the dramatic role the Plains tribes played in American history. The Plains chieftains Sitting Bull, Crazy Horse, and Red Cloud are imprinted in our memory, as are the tragic debacles at the Little Bighorn ("Custer's Last Stand") and Wounded Knee, both of which involved the Indians of the Plains, the last tribes to resist U.S. government domination. Their very names—the Cheyenne, the Blackfeet, the Comanche, the Crow, the Arapaho, and, best known of all, the Sioux (or, as they called themselves, the Dakota), among many others—are some of the most familiar to our ears.

Nearly a century ago, their traditional way of life vanished forever. The descendants of the buffalo hunters and tepee dwellers of the old West now reside on reservations or have been assimilated into general American culture. By constructing the diorama in this book, you will create a pictorial record of Plains Indian life as it was before these devastating changes, at the time best known to non-Indians: the early nineteenth century. That was after the Plains tribes had begun to enjoy certain advantages brought by white pioneers, particularly the horse, introduced to America by the Spanish in the sixteenth century. The early nineteenth century was also a time when these Indian hunters were still free to roam the Plains in search of the one animal essential to their culture: the American bison or "buffalo." At that time the buffalo, later hunted to near-extinction (a fate from which they have been rescued in this century), still crossed the Plains in vast herds, as shown on the second of the two backgrounds provided for this diorama (**Plate** 10). Most Plains tribes were nomadic like the buffalo they hunted; they occupied no permanent

dwelling sites but lived in temporary camps of tents called tepees—the kind of Indian dwelling most familiar to non-Indians. The first diorama background (**Plate** 1) depicts a typical tepee camp.

Plate 1

Among the Plains Indians, the men ruled the tribe's activities in hunting and war, but the women were not without considerable influence and authority in the domestic sphere. Theirs was also the responsibility of setting up and dismantling the tepees. The process of erecting a tepee— shown on this plate (left)—involved the following steps. The women arranged several wooden poles in a circle, leaned them against one another, and lashed them together at the top. This foundation was covered with several buffalo hides that had been sewn together. An opening was left at the top to allow the smoke of indoor fires to escape. Flaps attached to poles permitted the opening to be covered in bad weather.

At the left, a horse carries a bundle on a *travois*, a device consisting of two poles tied together at the front end and another piece fastened across the middle. The travois was tied to a horse or dog, the two poles simply dragging on the ground behind. It was the Plains Indians' principal mode of transporting their belongings from one campsite to another (see also **Plate** 14). Before the Europeans brought the horse, the dog served as their only draft animal. Oddly, although they readily adopted the horse, they were much slower to adopt wheeled vehicles, also brought by Europeans. Yet they freely employed such objects as the iron pot being used for cooking by the squaw (center) and the woven fabrics used for some garments. Plains Indians, unlike some other tribes, did not weave their own fabrics, and most did not make their own pottery.

The three warriors conversing in the foreground belong to the same society. Men, and often women, belonged to various clubs, societies, or associations. These served various secular and religious, civil and military purposes and were of the highest importance in the social life of the tribe.

At the right a woman scrapes a buffalo hide, and another hangs up

text continues on the inside back cover

TERRITORY OF THE PLAINS INDIANS

TEPEE CAMP: BACKGROUND

Plate 1

Plate 2

INNER LEFT SIDE

LEFT SIDE PANEL

OUTER LEFT SIDE

RIGHT SIDE PANEL

OUTER RIGHT SIDE

INNER RIGHT SIDE

Plate 3

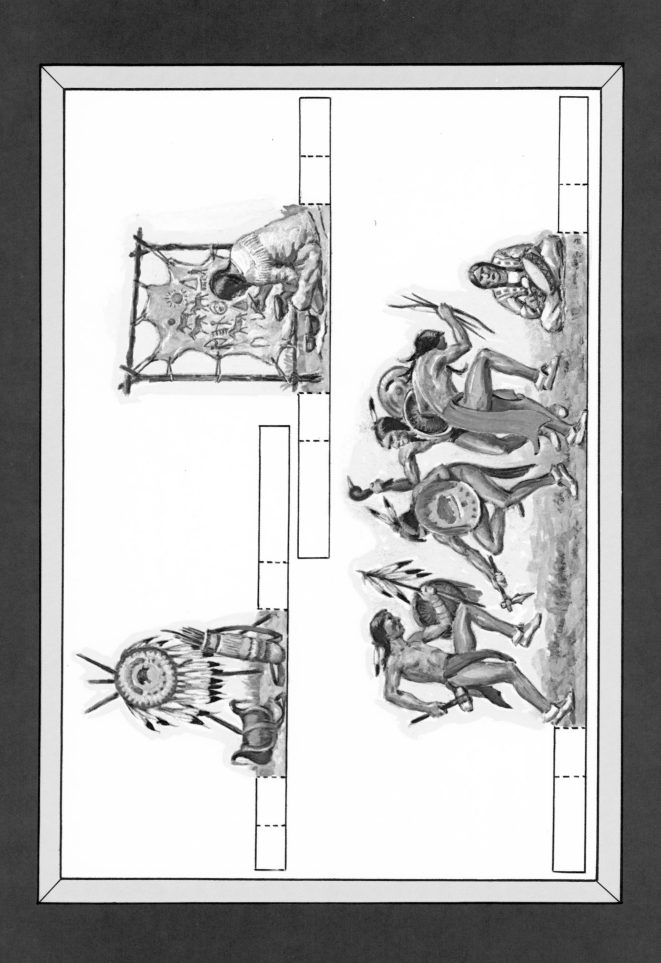

Plate 4

FRONT PANEL; TEPEE CAMP: CUTOUTS

BACK BRACE

FRONT BRACE

FLOOR

Plate 5

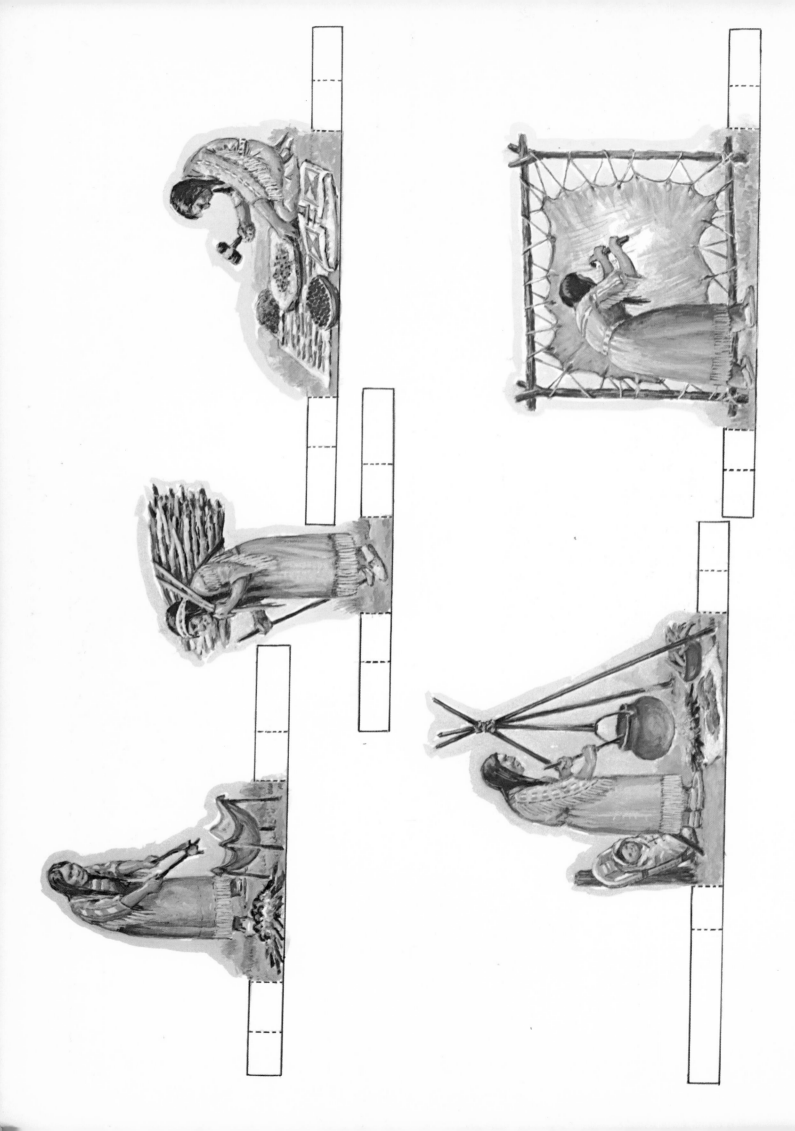

Plate 6

TEPEE CAMP: FIGURES

TEPEE CAMP: FIGURES

Plate 7

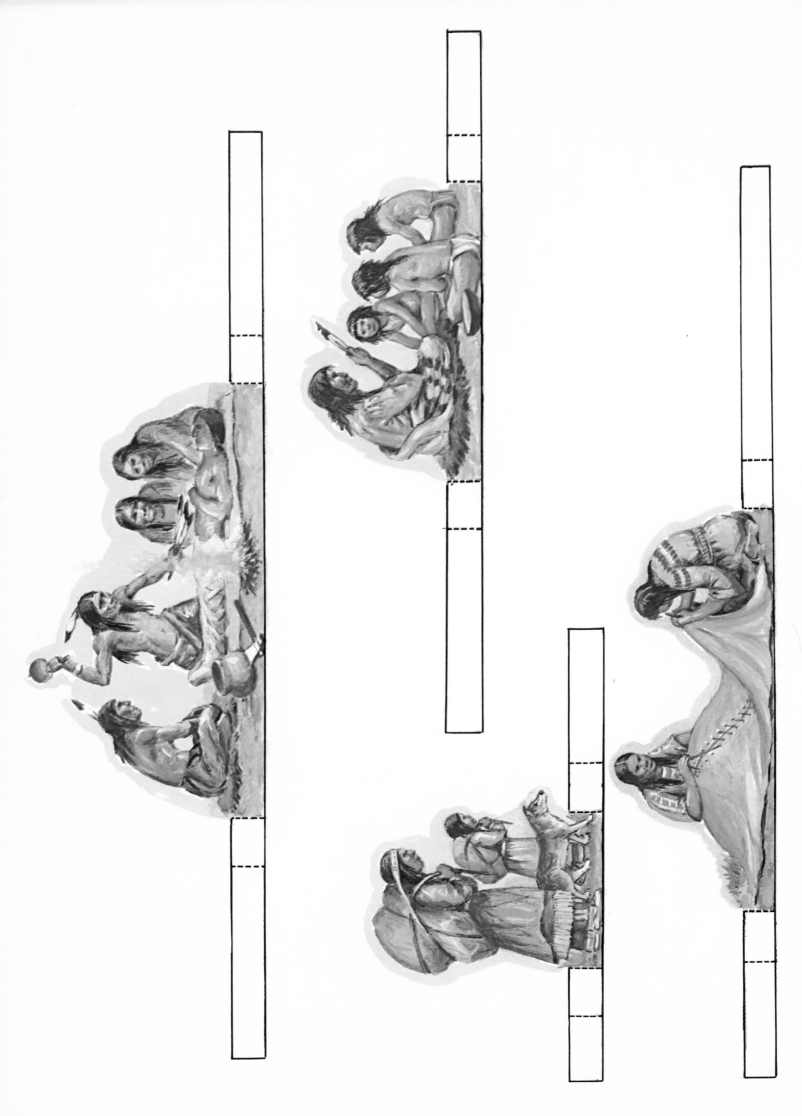

Plate 8

TEPEE CAMP: FIGURES

TEPEE CAMP: FIGURES

Plate 9

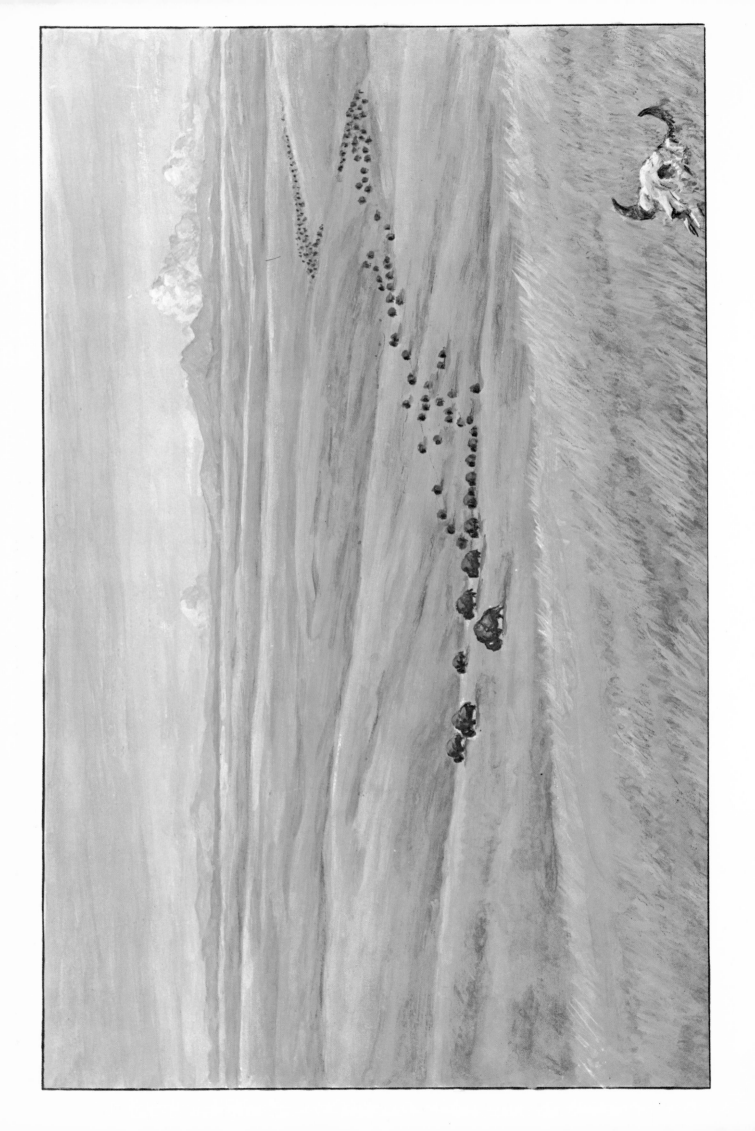

Plate 10

BUFFALO HUNT: BACKGROUND

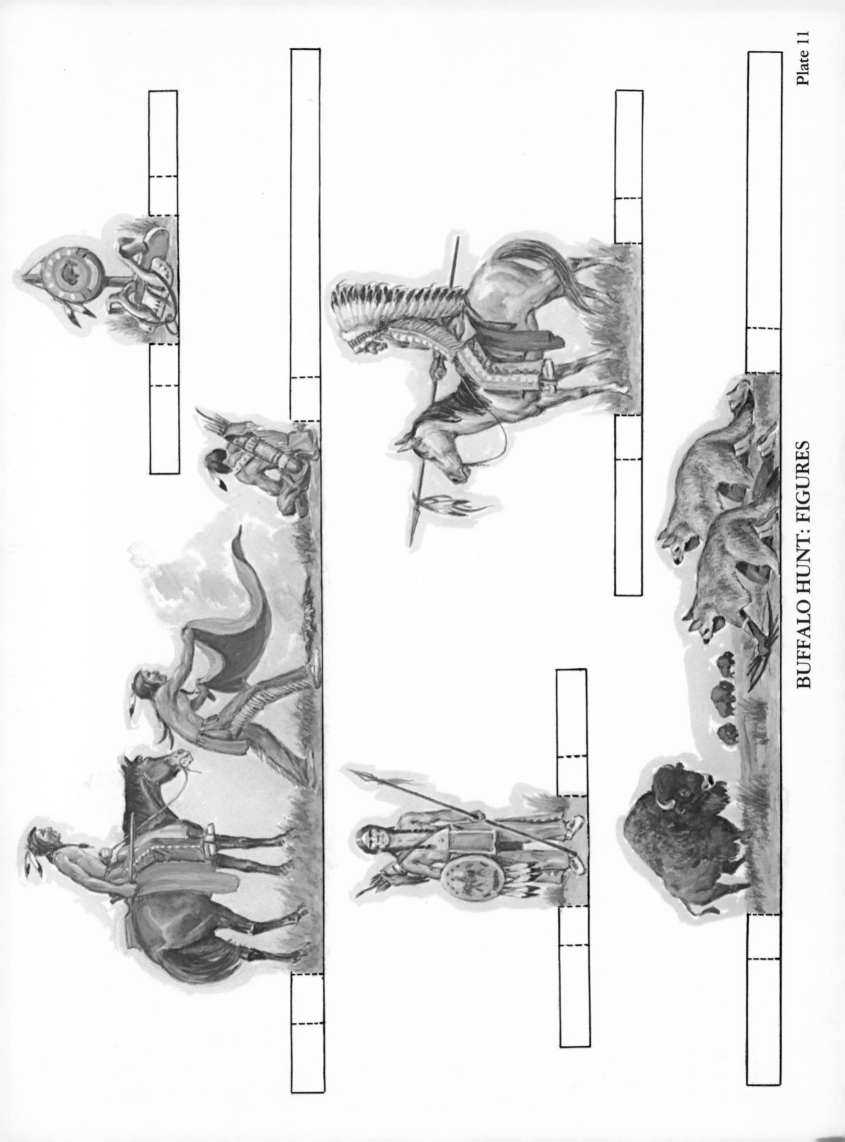

Plate 11

BUFFALO HUNT: FIGURES

BUFFALO HUNT: CUTOUTS

Plate 12

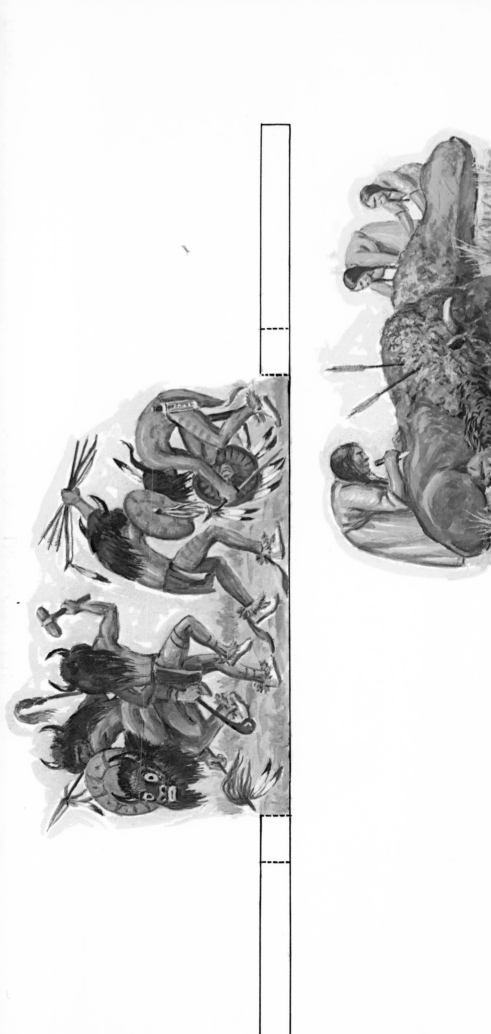

BUFFALO HUNT: CUTOUTS

Plate 13